# Polar Regions
## Surviving in Antarctica

### by Sunita Apte

Consultant: Daniel H. Franck, Ph.D.

BEARPORT
PUBLISHING COMPANY, INC.

New York, New York

CREDITS
Cover, Robert Harding/Getty Images; Title page, Robert Harding/Getty Images; 4, yourexpedition.com; 5, yourexpedition.com; 6, Steve Stankiewitz; 7, Maria Stenzel/National Geographic Image Collection; 8, Corbis; 9, Wolfgang Kaehler/Corbis; 10(T), yourexpedition.com; 10(B), yourexpedition.com; 11, Steve Stankiewitz; 12, Gordon Wiltsie/National Geographic Image Collection; 13(T&B), yourexpedition.com; 14, PunchStock/Corbis; 15(T), K.A. Puttock/Getty Images; 15(B), PunchStock/Corbis; 16, yourexpedition.com; 17, yourexpedition.com; 18, yourexpedition.com; 19, yourexpedition.com; 20, yourexpedition.com; 21, yourexpedition.com; 22, Hubertus Kanus/Photo Researchers, Inc.; 23(T), yourexpedition.com; 23(B), Galen Rowell/Corbis; 24, Jonathan Berry/Stringer/AFP/Getty Images; 25 (T&B), Reuters/Corbis; 26, yourexpedition.com; 27, Reuters/Corbis.

EDITORIAL DEVELOPMENT by Judy Nayer
DESIGN AND PRODUCTION by Paula Jo Smith

*Library of Congress Cataloging-in-Publication Data*

Apte, Sunita.
  Polar regions : surviving in Antarctica / by Sunita Apte.
     p. cm. — (X-treme places)
  Includes bibliographical references and index.
  ISBN 1-59716-088-1 (lib. bdg.) — ISBN 1-59716-125-X (pbk.)
1. Bancroft, Ann—Travel—Antarctica—Juvenile literature. 2. Arnesen, Liv—Travel—Antarctica—Juvenile literature. 3. Antarctica—Description and travel—Juvenile literature. 4. Women adventurers—Antarctica—Juvenile literature. I. Title. II. Series.

G863.A68 2006
919.8'9—dc22

                    2005006611

For more information, write to Bearport Publishing Company, Inc., 101 Fifth Avenue, Suite 6R, New York, New York 10003. Printed in the United States of America.

1 2 3 4 5 6 7 8 9 10

# Contents

# Crossing Antarctica

It was February 14, 2001—Valentine's Day. Outside, the temperature was well below freezing. Snow and ice covered the ground. Inside their tent, Liv (LEEV) Arnesen and Ann Bancroft faced a difficult decision.

They had spent the past two months skiing across the **continent** of Antarctica. They had traveled over 1,700 miles (2,736 km) but still had almost 500 miles (805 km) to go. They weren't sure they could finish the trip before the harsh Antarctic winter set in.

**Liv Arnesen and Ann Bancroft inside their tent**

It was hard to think of stopping. This **expedition** had been Ann and Liv's dream since they were girls. Continuing on, however, meant risking their lives.

Antarctica has one of the most extreme climates on Earth. Ninety-eight percent of it is covered in ice. The lowest temperature on Earth, -129°F (-89°C), was recorded here.

Liv and Ann were trying to ski almost as many miles or kilometers as the distance from New York to Los Angeles.

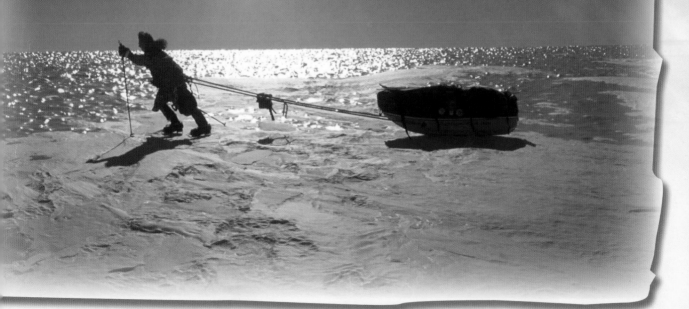

5

# The Top and Bottom of the World

Antarctica is located in one of Earth's two polar regions. These areas lie at the top and bottom of the world. At the top is the Arctic, or North Polar Region, which surrounds the North Pole. At the bottom is the Antarctic, or South Polar Region, which surrounds the South Pole.

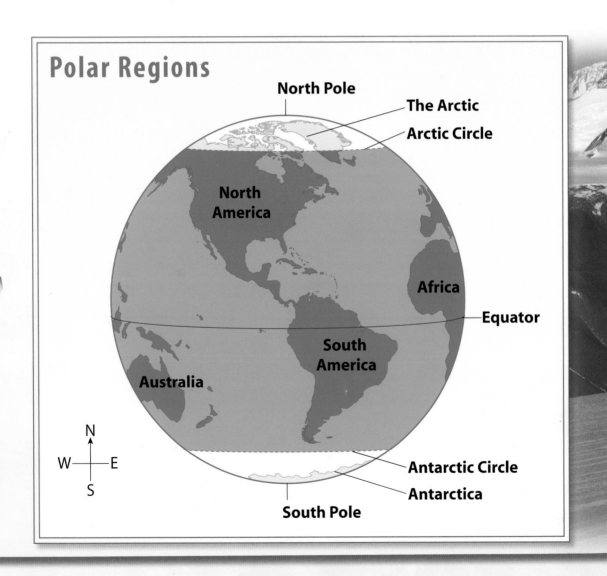

**Polar Regions**

North Pole

The Arctic

Arctic Circle

North America

Africa

Equator

South America

Australia

N
W — E
S

Antarctic Circle

Antarctica

South Pole

Antarctica is the world's coldest, windiest, and driest continent. People call it "the Ice" because ice covers almost all the land. Surprisingly, Antarctica receives less than two inches (5 cm) of rain or snow a year. Winds blow at speeds of up to 120 miles per hour (193 kph). Temperatures can be -30°F (-34°C)—in the summer!

**Antarctica is huge. It is bigger than the United States, Mexico, and Europe put together.**

The Arctic is mainly ocean surrounded by land. The Antarctic is mostly land surrounded by ocean.

# Chasing a Dream

Though Ann grew up in Minnesota and Liv grew up in Norway, they shared the same dream as young girls. They wanted to ski across Antarctica. Both were inspired by the amazing story of the **explorer** Sir Ernest Shackleton.

Shackleton's ship, the *Endurance*, got stuck in the ice just one day's journey from Antarctica. It remained stuck for over ten months before sinking.

In 1914, Shackleton and 27 other men set out on an expedition to Antarctica. Their ship became trapped in the ice and sank. The crew ended up on a **deserted** island. From there, Shackleton and four others sailed a lifeboat for over 800 miles (1,287 km) to get help. The crew was finally rescued, almost two years after the expedition had set out.

During a time when many explorers died in the Antarctic, all the members of Shackleton's expedition survived.

Shackleton's crew waited to be rescued on Elephant Island. They stayed there for 105 days, cold and starving.

# Starting the Journey

Ann and Liv planned their expedition carefully. They would have to survive in one of the world's most extreme places. It was **critical** that they have the right food, clothing, and equipment. Everything they needed was packed onto two sleds.

## Polar Survival Equipment

Polar adventurers need a lot of equipment to cross the ice and snow. Here is some of the special gear they use.

**Crampons, Ice Screws, and Climbing Ropes**—for climbing up and down hills on the ice

**Clothing**—several layers and a waterproof jacket and pants, to keep out the extreme cold

**Gloves**—to keep hands warm and dry

**Sleds**—to haul all the gear necessary for the trip

**Goggles**—to protect eyes from the sun's harmful rays, especially those reflecting off the snow

**Skis**—the best way to get around on the ice and snow

**Sails**—to attach to skis on windy days in order to move faster

**Tent and Sleeping Bags**—to stay warm and safe during freezing nights

**Sunblock**—to prevent serious sunburn caused by light reflecting off the ice

**GPS Receiver**—a positioning device to keep people from getting lost

On November 13, 2000, Liv and Ann were dropped off on "the Ice." As they said good-bye to the pilots, the two explorers knew they wouldn't see anyone else for months. Ann and Liv pointed their skis in the direction of the South Pole. They began their **mission** to become the first women to cross Antarctica.

## Liv and Ann's Trip

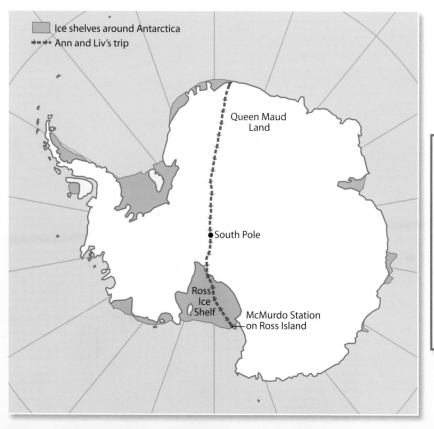

Ice shelves around Antarctica
Ann and Liv's trip

Queen Maud Land

South Pole

Ross Ice Shelf

McMurdo Station on Ross Island

**Liv and Ann started their trip in Queen Maud Land. They planned to end their trip at McMurdo Station, on the other side of Antarctica.**

Both Liv and Ann had been to Antarctica before. They had each skied to the South Pole.

# Antarctica's Geography

   Much of Antarctica is over 7,000 feet (2,134 m) high. Besides being cold, icy, and windy, Antarctica is high up. Mountain ranges cross the continent. Even where there are no mountains, thick ice sheets and rivers of ice called **glaciers** cover the surface.

Some mountain peaks, known as nunataks (NUN-uh-tahks), jut out of Antarctica's snow and ice.

Antarctica is the highest continent on Earth. The South Pole is about 9,300 feet (2,835 m) above sea level.

In their first three weeks on "the Ice," Ann and Liv climbed more than 10,000 feet (3,048 m) up the Sygyn Glacier. Pulling a 250-pound (113-kg) sled up a glacier for 12 hours a day wasn't easy. At such a high **altitude**, the air is very cold and thin. Ann and Liv found it hard to breathe. They got headaches and were exhausted at night.

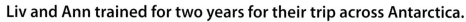

Liv and Ann trained for two years for their trip across Antarctica.

Part of Ann and Liv's route was covered with sastrugi (SAS-troo-gee). Sastrugi are frozen ice waves. They can be over ten feet (3 m) tall!

# Polar Wildlife

For most of their time on Antarctica, Liv and Ann had been alone in an empty land. They had seen birds, but no other animals. They hadn't passed any trees or plants. Almost nothing can survive the extreme **environment** of Antarctica's **interior**.

**Whales can be found in both the Arctic and the Antarctic.**

The Arctic contains much more wildlife than the Antarctic. It is home to polar bears, foxes, reindeer, and other animals.

It is different, however, on the coast. The cold ocean water around the continent is full of fish and tiny animals called krill. During warmer months, seals, penguins, and whales enjoy this plentiful food. Once winter comes, however, many of the animals leave. Only one type of seal and two kinds of penguins stay on Antarctica's coast all year long.

Weddell seals are the only seals that live on Antarctica all year long. Like whales, seals have an extra layer of body fat, called blubber, to keep them warm.

Over 100 million penguins live on Antarctica.

# Staying in Touch

Though Liv and Ann journeyed alone on Antarctica, they managed to keep in touch with the outside world. Before leaving, the women had set up a Web site for their expedition. Almost every day, they posted updates on the site by **satellite phone**.

**Liv and Ann took turns broadcasting messages from Antarctica on their Web site.**

As teachers, Liv and Ann were **passionate** about sharing their journey with children. They wanted kids to have the experience of "riding along in their sleds" with them. They got their wish. Millions of schoolchildren followed Liv and Ann's journey. The letters the women received from these students kept them from being lonely.

Schoolchildren in 46 countries followed Ann and Liv's expedition on the Internet.

# Finally, the South Pole!

Journeying across "the Ice" required mental and physical toughness. The women faced terrible weather and long, dangerous **treks**. They were worried, too. They weren't traveling fast enough.

Ann and Liv had sails to catch the wind so they could travel more quickly. However, on the world's windiest continent, they hadn't seen much wind. Most days, Liv and Ann traveled less distance than they expected and soon fell behind.

On a windy day, Liv and Ann could cover up to 65 miles (105 km) of flat ground with their sails. On skis alone, they traveled only five to ten miles (8 to 16 km) a day.

At last, on January 16, 2001, Ann and Liv made it to the South Pole. They had traveled 1,300 miles (2,092 km). After 64 days, they were thrilled to see other people. They didn't stay long, though. Ahead lay 900 miles (1,448 km) to cover in very little time.

**Liv and Ann at the South Pole**

# A Difficult Decision

Almost a month later, on February 12, Liv and Ann completed the crossing of Antarctica's land mass. They had become the first women to ski across Antarctica—an amazing **feat**. However, they still had almost 500 miles (805 km) to go to finish their journey. As winter approached, the weather would worsen. Soon a plane wouldn't be able to land to rescue them. If they got **stranded** on the ice, they could die.

**Ann outside her tent**

Like Shackleton in 1909, Liv and Ann weighed the odds. Taking chances on "the Ice" could be deadly. So, with heavy hearts, the women decided to end their expedition.

**This plane picked up Ann and Liv to begin their journey home.**

**The North and South poles have opposite seasons. When it's summer in Antarctica, it's winter in the Arctic.**

# Researchers on Ice

Liv and Ann had hoped to make it to the McMurdo **Research** Station to end their journey. This station is one of many set up in Antarctica. A number of countries have research stations on the continent. Most are only up and running for the summer. Just a few stations, such as Amundsen-Scott and McMurdo, stay open all year.

The people who stay on Antarctica during the winter are trapped there. Since planes can't land, they have no way to get off the continent.

McMurdo is the biggest year-round station in Antarctica.

A few hundred people live at the research stations year-round. Winter life on a station is tough. There isn't a lot of fresh food. No one can spend much time outside, where it's dark almost 24 hours a day.

One danger of living in Antarctica is frostbite. Frostbite happens when hands, feet, noses, and other parts of the body freeze solid.

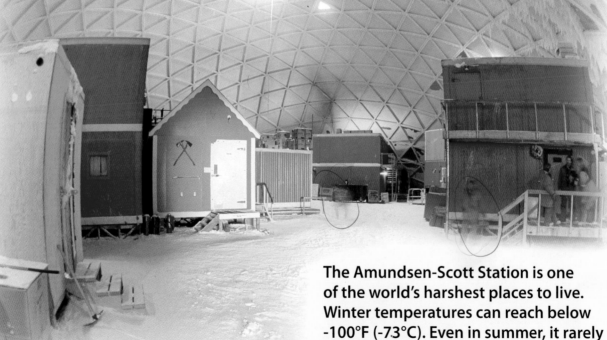

The Amundsen-Scott Station is one of the world's harshest places to live. Winter temperatures can reach below -100°F (-73°C). Even in summer, it rarely gets warmer than 0°F (-18°C).

# Will Antarctica Survive?

Many scientists come to Antarctica's stations to do research. They study the land, animals, and climate. Antarctica's land and ice hold clues that help scientists learn about Earth's distant past. The animals that live there show scientists how creatures are **adapted** to the cold. Scientists study how Antarctica's climate affects weather all over the globe.

Antarctica's clear air makes it a great place to study the sky. Lucky visitors can see the southern lights, a colorful nighttime display.

Lately, Antarctica's climate has some scientists worried. **Global warming** seems to be making parts of the continent warmer. Glaciers and **ice shelves** are melting. If too much ice melts, it could mean huge problems. Sea levels would rise. Coastlines around the world would flood.

**Larsen B ice shelf collapsing**

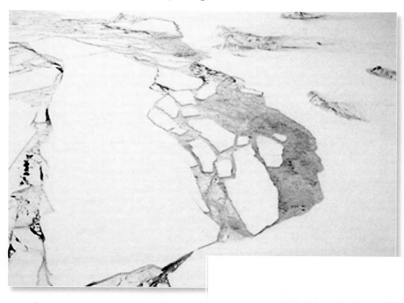

Antarctica's **peninsula** is getting warmer. In 2002, an ice shelf called the Larsen B collapsed.

# Back into the Cold

After Ann and Liv made the decision to stop their journey, a plane picked them up and flew them to McMurdo. From there, they boarded a boat for the trip home.

Like almost everyone who spends time on "the Ice," these two explorers care passionately about the future of Antarctica. They know that Earth's polar regions are changing fast. They try to share this message with others.

**After 94 days and 1,717 miles (2,763 km), Ann and Liv were happy to be off "the Ice."**

Ann and Liv's Antarctic expedition made people more aware of the world's coldest continent. Next, they would focus on the top of the world. In February 2005, Ann and Liv set off on skis again—across the Arctic.

**Liv and Ann on their way home.**

**Learn more about Liv and Ann's polar expeditions at their Web site: www.yourexpedition.com/.**

# Just the Facts

## MORE ABOUT POLAR REGIONS AND LIV AND ANN'S EXPEDITION

- The Antarctic is actually a cold desert.

- The Antarctic is much colder than the Arctic. The average winter temperature in the Antarctic is about -76°F (-60°C). The Arctic's average winter temperature is -30°F (-34°C).

- Polar regions have only two seasons, summer and winter. In summer, the sun never really sets at the South and North poles. It's light outside 24 hours a day. During the winter, the sun never really rises. It is dark all the time.

# Timeline

**This timeline shows some important events in the history of Antarctic exploration.**

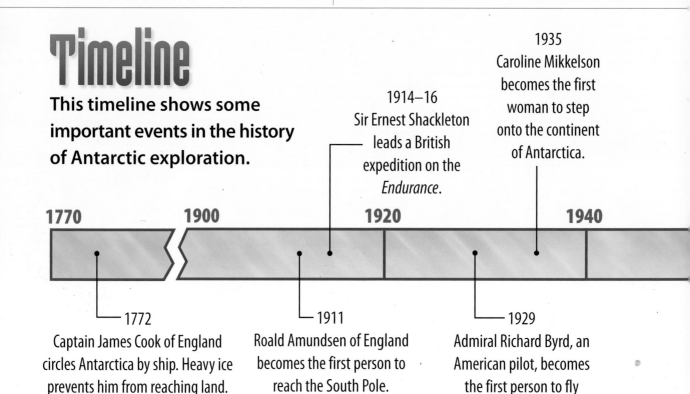

**1914–16**
Sir Ernest Shackleton leads a British expedition on the *Endurance*.

**1935**
Caroline Mikkelson becomes the first woman to step onto the continent of Antarctica.

**1770**     **1900**     **1920**     **1940**

**1772**
Captain James Cook of England circles Antarctica by ship. Heavy ice prevents him from reaching land.

**1911**
Roald Amundsen of England becomes the first person to reach the South Pole.

**1929**
Admiral Richard Byrd, an American pilot, becomes the first person to fly across the South Pole.

- Except for a few hundred people at the research stations, no one lives in the Antarctic year-round—it's too cold. In the Arctic, however, about two million people live inside the Arctic Circle.

- Before the trip, Ann and Liv trained as many as six hours a day to build up their strength. They skied, kayaked, hiked, and wind-sailed. They also hauled tires and chopped wood!

- Skiing is hard work and burns up a lot of calories. During the journey, Ann and Liv ate high-energy foods rich in fat. These foods included chocolate, caramels, and potato chips.

- Because Antarctica can be so windy, Liv and Ann had to make sure that nothing blew away. Each night, they tied all their gear together and staked it to the ground.

- It was so cold inside Ann and Liv's tent that they cooked while sitting in their sleeping bags.

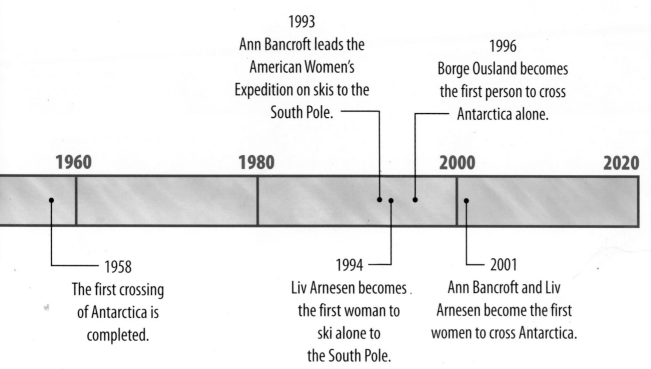

1993
Ann Bancroft leads the American Women's Expedition on skis to the South Pole.

1996
Borge Ousland becomes the first person to cross Antarctica alone.

1960    1980    2000    2020

1958
The first crossing of Antarctica is completed.

1994
Liv Arnesen becomes the first woman to ski alone to the South Pole.

2001
Ann Bancroft and Liv Arnesen become the first women to cross Antarctica.

# GLOSSARY

**adapted** (uh-DAP-tid) changed because of the environment; changed over time to be fit for the environment

**altitude** (al-ti-TOOD) the height above sea level

**continent** (KON-tuh-nuhnt) one of the world's seven large land masses

**critical** (KRIT-uh-kuhl) very important, a matter of life and death

**deserted** (di-ZUR-tid) having no people living in an area

**environment** (en-VYE-ruhn-muhnt) the plants, animals, and weather in a place

**expedition** (ek-spuh-DISH-uhn) a long journey taken for a reason, such as exploring

**explorer** (ek-SPLOR-uhr) someone who travels in order to discover something new

**feat** (FEET) an action requiring strength, courage, or both

**glaciers** (GLAY-shurz) huge areas of ice and snow found on mountains and near the North and South poles

**global warming** (GLOHB-uhl WARM-ing) a rise in temperatures around the world

**ice shelves** (EYESS SHELVZ) masses of ice that are attached to land but jut out to sea

**interior** (in-TIHR-ee-ur) inside, away from the coast or edge

**mission** (MISH-uhn) an important job or task

**passionate** (PASH-uh-nit) caring very deeply

**peninsula** (puh-NIN-suh-luh) land surrounded by water on three sides

**research** (re-SURCH or REE-surch) the collecting of information

**satellite phone** (SAT-uh-*lite* FOHN) a mobile phone that uses a satellite, or a communications spacecraft, to send and receive calls

**stranded** (STRAN-did) stuck somewhere without a way to leave

**treks** (TREKS) long, often difficult hikes

# BIBLIOGRAPHY

**Billings, Henry.** *Antarctica: Enchantment of the World.* Chicago, IL: Children's Press (1994).

**Rohter, Larry.** "Antarctica, Warming, Looks Ever More Vulnerable." *The New York Times* (January 25, 2005).

**Williams, Jack.** *The Complete Idiot's Guide to the Arctic and the Antarctic.* New York: Alpha Books (2003).

**Willis, Clint, ed.** *Ice: Stories of Survival from Polar Exploration.* New York: Adrenaline Books (1999).

**www.yourexpedition.com/**

# READ MORE

**Dewey, Jennifer Owings.** *Antarctic Journal: Four Months at the Bottom of the World.* New York: HarperCollins (2001).

**Poncet, Sally.** *Antarctic Encounter: Destination South Georgia.* New York: Simon & Schuster (1995).

**Taylor, Barbara.** *Arctic and Antarctic.* New York: Knopf (1995).

# LEARN MORE ONLINE

Visit these Web sites to learn more about Liv and Ann, their expeditions, and polar regions:

**astro.uchicago.edu/cara/vtour/**

**www.arctic.noaa.gov/gallery_np.html**

**www.bancroftarnesenexplore.com/**

# INDEX

# ABOUT THE AUTHOR

Sunita Apte is a children's book author living in Brooklyn, New York. When she's not writing books for kids, she likes to cook and travel to extreme places. She has long dreamed of going to Antarctica.